This is the catalogue of the exhibition

**The Probable Causes
of Future Experience**

25 April–1 May 2019

The Darkroom,
32 North Brunswick St.,
Stoneybatter, Dublin 7
Ireland

Between Four Walls

Yvonne Higgins

Published by **The Onslaught Press**
19A Corso Street, Dundee, DD2 1DR
on 1 April 2019

Images © 2019 **Yvonne Higgins**

Design & this edition © 2019 **Mathew Staunton**

All rights reserved. No part of this publication may be reproduced, stored in a retrieval system, or transmitted, in any form or by any means, electronic, mechanical, photocopying, recording, or otherwise, without the prior permission in writing of the publisher, or as expressly permitted by law, or under terms agreed with the appropriate reprographics rights organization

ISBN: **978-1-912111-95-4**

The text is set in **Helvetica** and Le Monde Livre

Printed & bound by Lightning Source On Demand Services

We level mountains, fell trees, tame animals. Settlements keep on increasing where before there were only swamps and forests. We put people all at once in new lands.

We have subdued the world; metal and beasts have become servants. We have enslaved the coloured races, crudely organised the relationship between nations and tamed the masses. Justice is still a distant thing. There's more hurt and misery.

Childish doubts and apprehensions seem unimportant.

Janusz Korczak
(The Child's Right to Respect, 1929)

Contents

8 **Preface** Mathew Staunton & Ian Joyce

Exhibition pieces

26 Fitting in a Burrow
28 Be Firm
30 Caution Children
32 Gabriel's Gift
34 Falling
36 Delivery
38 Croup
40 Castaway
42 Hideout
44 On the Edge
46 Timeout
48 It'll Pass Off
50 Revival
52 Daydream
54 Swing
56 The Judgement of Judy
58 Changeling

17 Poems

- 62 **Until the Spider Returns** Nisha Bhakoo
- 63 **what he will always remember** Steve Pottinger
- 64 **Haiku** Gabriel Rosenstock
- 65 **Woman-power** Tim Quinlan
- 66 **Untitled** Michel Jovet
- 67 **Revelation** Tim Quinlan
- 68 **The Empty Chair** Rethabile Masilo
- 69 **History** Athol Williams
- 70 **Oubliette** Jazmine Linklater
- 71 **Untitled** Alan John Stubbs
- 72 **Jackson in The Pasadena Hills** Ingrid Casey
- 73 **Chair** Ian Joyce
- 74 **Jack and The Flying Deer** Emilio Higgins Gentile
- 75 **Shapeshifter** Jackie Gorman
- 76 **Birdie** Matt Barnard
- 77 **Untitled** Alison Bown
- 78 **Océane** Aoife Staunton

80 Biographies

Preface

Mathew Staunton & Ian Joyce

1

Thinking about children is thinking about relative powerlessness, slavery and the N word.

John Lennon and Yoko Ono counter visualized the role of women in their 1972 single **Woman is the Nigger of the World** making a strong claim for the right to look differently. Controversially, the N word was now supposed to expand to include all oppressed peoples, with women projected as the most oppressed group worldwide. Using this linguistic strategy interviewers[1] and audiences alike were provoked into questioning the appropriateness and relevance of the argument by referencing the taboo nature of the subject itself. It gave John and Yoko myriad opportunities to bottle their message. One element of the song that might still need unpacking for 1970s listeners was the couplet:

**Woman is the slave to the slave
Yeah, Connolly was right, we scream it**

With a very sparse number of references to the Irish Socialist and Republican leader James Connolly, UK and US television fans of the Plastic Ono Band would not have immediately recognised the citation:

**The worker was the slave of capitalist society,
the female worker is the slave of that slave**[2]

The utter powerlessness of women in the capitalist system (they had no control over how the value of their labour was calculated and are still undervalued today) is reimagined by Connolly who places them in an underclass beneath even that of the slave in the class hierarchy. What could be lower than the slave of a slave?

In 1954, Jacques Brel offered examples of the lowest of the low in **Ne me Quitte Pas**. In this world famous song he visualizes

---

1. Apple Records used a statement by black Congressman Ron Dellums to demonstrate the broader use of the term in a **Billboard** magazine ad on 6 May

2. in P. Beresford Ellis (ed.), **James Connolly— Selected Writings**, p. 191.

what eclipsing entirely his male identity would look like, were he to convince his beloved to please, please, please stay with me. Listen to the extreme lengths he will go to:

Je ne vais plus pleurer
Je ne vais plus parler
Je me cacherai là
À te regarder danser et sourire et
À t'écouter chanter et puis rire
Laisse-moi devenir l'ombre de ton ombre
L'ombre de ta main
L'ombre de ton chien

He won't cry. He won't talk. He will hide himself. He will watch. He will listen . . . as the woman takes centre stage, singing and laughing. Now, if woman is the slave to a slave then what would the shadow of her shadow look like? Or the shadow of her hand? What would the shadow of her dog be worth? This is what the desperation of the desperate character who narrates Brel's song is prepared to become. He will abase himself. Completely, reduce himself, pulp himself down to a status far, far, beneath that of the woman he adores. As far beneath as the abandonment of his power as a man and everything else that goes with it can bare, further in fact. Frank Sinatra offers only to be the shadow of the woman's dog in **If You Go Away**, the English version. His argument does not go anywhere near as far as Brel's but is no less surreal for all that, with a social mobility that reaches the lows of a rung of the ladder that is as high as a dog's shadow (below nowhere at all). His desperation is similarly beyond the beyond and further again.

Perhaps the most pathetic cover version of the song is Nina Simone's 1965 in French! The spectacle of an African-American woman singing with considerable difficulty in a foreign language about how to be the shadow of a man's shadow, or the shadow of a man's hand reflects the lived experience of women at the time—in a way that Brel's and Sinatra's fantasies fail to reflect men's situation in real life. What was a migrant black woman worth in 1965? This was the same year Jim Crow laws were abandoned in the Southern United States and signs decreeing **No Blacks, No Dogs, No Irish** still laid down the de facto rules determining who could live where in the UK.

In the 1960s, ranking people in hierarchies according to their colour and sex and structuring such social hierarchies was aestheticized as good and proper by many in the anglo-saxon world. Counter-visual resistance was already underway. The hegemonic Visuality (Bunracht na hÉireann, Jim Crow, Apartheid) resisted this resistance, mutating and developing new strategies to better maintain authority and the status quo. Both Jacques Brel's and Nina Simone's very different versions of **Ne Me Quitte Pas** have as much force today, perhaps even more than they ever did. The time when a man and a woman would have to lose the same amount of privilege to become the shadow of a dog is still a long way away.

We haven't touched rock bottom yet, however. That position is reserved for children.

Children do not register in the eye of history. They are voiceless statistics. In the media they are objects, symbols for the brutality of war, famine and genocide. They arouse sympathy and humanise events and ministers or, like cat videos, they provide adults with cute entertainment. They are rarely given a voice and their views are not taken seriously when they are.

Children, like slaves, are minors. They can't vote, even on issues that concern only children, enjoy no agency, and have had to suffer centuries of adults justifying a wide range of cruel acts developed and passed down from generation to generation of parents and teachers to keep them under control. The adult gaze visualizes children as weak, in need of protection, volatile, apolitical, unopinionated and powerless while aestheticizing physical punishment as necessary.

Fitz-James O'Brien's 1859 science fiction/horror story **What Was It? A Mystery** illustrates what the extreme powerlessness of the small and socially invisible can lead to in a socierty organised around hierarchies of value.

Ostensibly, it tells the tale of a pair of clueless American bachelors living in a Manhattan boarding house in the 1850s. After rebuffing what they perceive as a surprise attack by an invisible strangler, they tie it up and wring their hands for several weeks as it starves to death. The narrator, Harry Escott, claims that he has tried everything to keep his captive alive but not once does he consider releasing it or calling in outside help. Here is a description of the creature's death:

> Ten, twelve days, a fortnight passed, and it still lived. The pulsations of the heart, however, were daily growing fainter, and had now nearly ceased altogether. It was evident that the creature was dying for want of sustenance. (. . .) At last, it died. Hammond and I found it cold and stiff one morning in bed. The heart had ceased to beat, the lungs to inspire. We hastened to bury it in the garden. It was a strange funeral, the dropping of that viewless corpse into the damp hole.[3]

3. O'Brien, Fitz-James, **What Was It**, in **Seeing the Unseen**, Oxford, 2014, p.20

Crucially, there are no repercussions for either of the men because nobody cares about the fate of their victim. The word "victim" is used very deliberately here because without the intervention of Escott and his friend, the creature would not be dead at the end of the story. O'Brien has his narrator describe it as **small, not over four feet and some inches in height** and weighing about the same as a fourteen-year old boy. For Kristine Hoyt-Jouanne, this detail is the key to understanding the tale. She convincingly links the diminuitive size of the invisible being to the 1859 United States Supreme Court decision that confirmed and generalized the notion that slaves were property and the **Three Fifths Compromise** that counted them as a fraction of a human being for electoral purposes.[4] The creature is a minor in this respect but it also has the attributes of a child and this tale is, therefore, a narrative of abuse. Two middle-class, anglo-Saxon men torture and kill a being that is smaller and weaker but otherwise not very different from themselves and get away with it scot-free because it is invisible. In one of the very first tales to feature an invisible character, invisibility is presented as a very definite curse.

If O'Brien's creature is a then minor it is doubly invisible—physically impossible to see and socially invisible in a world that choses not to see slaves and children. Ralph Ellison describes how this social invisibility works in **Invisible Man**. His mechanism for not seeing black people works even better for children. It is

a peculiar disposition of the eyes of those with whom [the child] comes into contact. A matter of the construction of their inner eyes, those eyes with which they look through their physical eyes upon reality.[5]

This is no anatomical anomaly. Perception is not a natural attribute. It is a social activity, learned and cultivated. We perceive only what is deemed worthy of our attention and push all that is not into the background. Children are socially and historically invisible, unless politicians deem it necessary to kiss them or point at their misery in front of the cameras. The child is the true **nigger of the world** and always has been.

This is the subject of Ursula K. Le Guin's award-winning story **The Ones Who Walked away from Omelas**[6], first published in 1973. Omelas is a joyful, guilt-free, bright-towered city functioning perfectly without a monarchy, slavery, soldiers, advertising, secret police or bombs. Everyone is happy. This happiness, however,

4. Hoyt-Jouanne, Kristine, **How Much of a Man is Three Fifths of a Man**, in **Seeing the Unseen**, Oxford: Onslaught Press 2014, pp.47-66

5. Ellison Ralph, **Invisible Man**, New York: Vintage, 1952, p.3.

6. Originally published in **New Dimensions 3**, a science fiction anthology edited by Robert Silverberg, in October 1973. It was reprinted in Le Guin's **The Wind's Twelve Quarters** in 1975,

depends on an abominable contract that condemns a child to suffer in a windowless basement room, three paces long by two paces wide. The child is naked, **its buttocks and thighs are a mass of festered sores, and it sits in its own excrement continuously**. Everyone in Omelas learns about this contract when they are between eight and twelve years old and most of the Omelites who come to see the child in its room are young. They feel anger, rage and impotence at first but, over time, they learn to deal with the situation, control their feelings and accept this hideous reality. Eventually, they learn to be happy and push the abused child to the backs of their minds. They are gentle with their own children.

Occasionally, though, one of the young visitors to the child's room doesn't go home afterwards. They walk out of the city and don't come back. Sometimes a much older man or woman falls silent for a few days and then leaves home in a similar fashion.

Unsurprisingly, readers tend to identify with the Omelites who walk away. Le Guin gently pushes us in this direction internally by naming the story after them and, externally, by indicating that the hero of a later short story, the anarchist leader in **The Day Before the Revolution**[7], is one of those who walked away.

In a 1991 essay, however, American Professor Kenneth M. Roemer controversially challenges this reading and argues that it is on the people who stay in Omelas and succeed in performing grand acts of compassion and beauty despite their full knowledge of the contract, that we should be focusing our attention[8]. Why can't we readers, who exist in a similar world, do the same? He asks.

Walking away is a potentially revolutionary act, an act of defiance and social transformation by a person refusing to internalise the perversion of the social contract and the notion that ends

---

7. Published in 1974 this story represents an idealized anarchy by following the character of Odo, the legendary woman who led the revolution that founded the anarchist society in **The Dispossessed**

8. **The Talking Porcupine Liberates Utopia: Le Guin's "Omelas" as Pretext to the Dance** in **Utopian Studies** 2 (1/2):6-18 (1991)

justify means. But it is clearly not an easy option. It means losing a home, a family and a way of life, because the world as it is is unacceptable.

Like Roemer, though, we believe that Le Guin is trying to trick us, even for a split second, into identifying with those who stay and rationalise the situation. The description of the abusive treatment of the child is so realistically horrible that no amount of beauty, art and gaiety should be able to cancel it out and this posits a very disturbing question: what sort of community could accept such a hideous deal and live happily and guilt-free in spite of it?

Le Guin forces us to ask ourselves if we have ever made or could live with such a deal and in what circumstances we will accept the maltreatment of children? How would Irish teachers, the Garda Síochána, the Pope, Barack Obama, Donald Trump, Benjamin Netanyahu, the British Conservative and Labour Parties, Barbara Streisand, Emmanuel Macron and Mark Zuckerberg answer this question? Unfortunately, encouraged by our politicians and our media, we can and often do find ingenious ways to justify maltreatment and murder. And this is where the voicelessness of children is most obvious. How would a child answer the same question? Could he or she imagine a scenario in which it would be acceptable to torture, abuse or kill another child? They are never asked such important questions in meaningful or binding contexts. Occasionally, they can choose the colour of a Cadbury's wrapper in a focus group but they never get to vote on whether or not collateral damage should be tolerated in and around drone strikes. Their opinions on corporal punishment in schools and homes are never surveyed. And they are not asked if they want to be baptised into a church that has consistently failed to safeguard their peers. These are decisions that are made by adults and justifed in ways that satisfy adult consciences.

In the first four decades of the 20th century, Polish doctor and pedagogue Janusz Korczak (1879-1942) took a radically different stance and completely reenvisioned the rights of children. He believed that children should have both respect and agency and introduced a democratic structure into the orphanage he directed in Warsaw, giving the children a say in all decisions. This **Children's Republic** had a parliament, a newspaper and a flag. It also had its own code of justice with a court established among the children to deal with perceived injustices.[9] Punishments generally consisted of asking for forgiveness. In August 1942, he refused to abandon the children and take avantage of multiple offers to save his own life when the Nazis decided to exterminate them. He walked with 192 children and his co-workers from the orphanage to the Treblinka death camp under the flag of the Children's Republic and they were all murdered together.

Here are the lines that follow those in the epigraph on page 5:

The child is not a soldier; he does not defend his homeland although he suffers together with it.

Since he has no vote, why go to the trouble to gain his good opinion of you? He doesn't threaten, demand, say anything.

Weak, little, poor, dependent—a citizen-to-be only. Indulgent, rude, brutal—but always indifferent.

The brat. Only a child, a future person, but not yet, not today. He's just going to be.

He has to be watched, never to be let out of sight; to be watched and never be left alone; watched at every step.

He may fall, bump himself, get hurt, get dirty, spill, tear, break, misplace, lose, set fire, leave the door open to burglars. He'll hurt himself and us; cripple himself, us, a playmate.

9. Korczak was tried by the children several times

We have to be vigilant, permit no independence of movement, be in full control.

The child does not know how much and what to eat, how much and what to drink, does not know the limits of fatigue. So, you have to supervise his diet, his sleep, his rest.

For how long? As of when? Always. Distrust changes with age; it does not diminish; rather, it even tends to increase.

He does not distinguish the important from the trivial. Order and systematic work are alien to him. He's absent-minded. He'll forget easily, treat lightly, neglect. He doesn't know anything about future responsibilities.

We have to instruct, guide, train, restrain, temper, correct, caution, prevent, impose, and combat. Combat whim, caprice, and obstinacy.

2

**Looking after Your Self
or Throwing Some light on Silence:**

We are all ears.

Sound is slower than the speed of light.

The story meanders, we follow suit, on a path that leads into a cul de sac, through a brick wall,

and out the other side . . . . through the picture frame.

Yvonne Higgins keeps herself on the far side of the "picture plane" . The image, so shocking and marvellous in Cocteau's film[10] is the "penetration of the mirror" at the outset. The access to Hades is the thread of the child's awareness. In Higgins's work, the potential (taking the image from classical physics) is working in the other direction, the return of a light which dims the closer you get to the surface. On my side of the canvas, I am calling out. Keep going, you are nearly there.

Her works work in slow motion, slowly teasing their way into our awareness.

Rather than dropping, the penny floats.

To "enjoy" looking at these works is not to leave off questioning what they are about.

It is to feel one's way gradually in the dark for what light remains in the picture frame.

Figuring out why this artist uses this genre to deal with "ambiguity" takes more than a cursory glance at the work.

The work itself points to its own prehistory.

10. **Orphée**, 1950.

The key is collage.

"Invented" by men in the 20th century, collage has existed since the invention of paper and was practised with pioneering gusto by Mary Delany in the 1770s[11]. It alienates. It juxtaposes. It creates beauty by making introductions on dissecting tables.

Higgins's work takes looking and looking again; "a looking" which is "a reading" and a reading which looks over and over, over and back, in and out, up and down, in series, in ones, and twos. Pictures that have left the exhibition behind, line up, separate out, recombine, hold hands, like a snaky line of school children on the streets of Paris on an outing from the École Maternelle.

A puzzle is a maze, is a labyrinth, is a claustrophobic airless vista, a chamber of ir-reality locked into the picture plane, a claustrophobic projection of the flat and flattened plane.

Are the works ambiguous or are they about ambiguity?

Are they full of knowingness or are they ambiguous about knowing??

Are they saying something about something unspoken?

What if nobody is listening?

Nobody looking?

Nobody watching?

Nobody to be seen?

Nobody even supposed to listen?

Turning a blind eye, and a deaf ear have something in common.

Turning a deaf ear to something invisible and a blind eye to a

11. Mary A. Delany, née Granville (1700–1788) was famous for her **paper mosaicks** in her lifetime but was historically invisible for much of the 20th century

voice of tenderness and self absorption is something else again.

Look again. Again look!!

Who am I?

I am No one. I am nobody. I have no body of my own.

Is the picture saying something?

Why can you not hear anything?

What is someone doing saying something through the picture?

Where does this come from?

You never "see me".

"You" never see "me"

If you can hear me, why can you not see me?

Am I pretending to hide?

Or am my hiding to pretend?

Why am I pretending?

Why am I not hiding?

Am I pretending not to be hurt or injured?

Or am I?

Am I for real?

Are my feelings for real?

Are my feelings fake?

In Art as in life, somebody is trying to say something, but in a language no one wants to be seen to understand. Saying something the old fashioned way, a shout of pain and suffering, a cry of "shame" is a cul de sac, a dead end. A blindness, not in the work, but in the eye of the beholder, a blind spot that makes shit happen

which this artist manages to bring into view . . . . in her estranged, estranging and quizzical works.

They seem to say "I don't need your gaze: I play in the privacy of the picture plane."

Art is dumb. You are blind.

This knowingness is the forbidden knowledge which each child carries over in to adulthood:

It is supposed to be left behind, buried in the "forgotten" childhood, licenced in the amnesia of adulthood . . . .

The chair is the site of the trouble and is a troubling pictorial presence.

This is the focus of the artists strategy as, a symbol of inexpressible difficulty which structuring these works as art entails. The trans-positioning that is in resistance to collapsing pressures of an experience which the works imply but do not— ever—bring into view.

This is a double act, the work assuming its interpretation and turns it on itself, like a reflection of a reflection that explodes the flat surface with a 3-dimensional object.

The chair, in these works is neither self-containing nor containable within the pictorial format as a static symbol.

It defies the "gravity" of a work of Art and escapes into a transition space, and hides, as it were, between reality and fiction, by overlooking or in fact, cleverly "looking over" and effacing the line that separates Art from reality.

This is not a line drawn in the sand, innocently and without awareness, but is the difficult, intentional and complex task of construction.

Collage is the appropriate and historical format that was taken up by the artist's forbears in the early 20th century, women artists like Hannah Hoch who invented the modern language of collage that was disseminated to, for example, Max Ernst.

Higgins's works combine a gentle self absorption of self regard, the tender self love that grows in a motherless self-mothering being, a being who finds itself alone and content in the space of its own imaginative making.

It is not the inheritance of the abused, but the disassociation of a new person, an identity as yet undefined, groping like the new born creature towards the light, out of darkness and the phantasmagoria of a hell left behind.

The moving element in the work is gentleness. This is consciously and cleverly disassociated from the what the work is about, leaving a aesthetic experience in the safely sealed off compartment of the "well made work"

The works can be seen, in series as growth, the stages of growth, intentionally deferring of a conventional "authorial" identity, not a search for style but a kind of suspension in an "anti-style" a depersonalised and neutralised construction of "style" full for pathos and a "thumbs up" lightness of touch.

3

I am alive. I am dead. Imagine! Mammy imagine! Imagine ME dead.

Smack my bottom. Smack my bottom. Be open about it. Smack my bottom in the open. Its in your nature to be open. Come out and let me have my bottom smacked in the open.

Into the dark without a light to light the way. Out of the dark into the light without a sign to sign the way. Children caution adults adults caution caution the blind leading the way hold my hand feel your way with me

Parthenogenisis

I am falling off, upwardly mobile. Its fun. I have a healthy psychology. I eat well, nature vomits. I spew my guts, no laughing matter, yellowed leaves. I am strict with myself. Team spirit. I am sure I can win lead, the Olympics are on the cards. Its a leap year

Parthenogenisis (again)

Croup, crop, group, grot, pour, pu, rou, roc . . .

I am flat as papyrus, my mother is a pain, i am afloat on the fame of a moses basket. I bask in reflected light of a sun gone out: A triumph of history over little ones that slosh around in the Jardin des Tuilieries.

Fuck Balthus—he left me in the Alps. Im sick of Art. I hate my class. I'd rather play with Alice and smoke the pipe of peace. It's late. I have had enough. Let's go to sleep.

I am on the edge on the edge am I

I am the philosopher turned to stone, time out in two dimensions, non plussed for good or ill

Don't pass me off as a life model. Pass me off as a pimp. Leave the toilet door ajar. I need to piss. I can't find my marbles. They must be here somewhere under the chair.

Zoology is my biology. I am a sucker for nature. Nature reserves are the stuff of dreams. Being outside in natural surroundings plays on her nerves. Mammy, what have you done with my stuffed toys?!

Concentrate. You are losing it. A hare or a rabbit. Big ears, big toes. Beady eyes, snub nose. Concentrate! A hare or a rabbit. Scaredey cat. A rabbit. A hare. A rabbit. A hare

Swing low sweet chariot. Swing low sweet chariot. Come for to carry me home.

Judy is a scarry ass. Judas Escariot. Punch and Judy. Luck of the draw. Draw on duck tape. Tie up her month. Put her in water. Swim for your life.

I am the sweets of no sin against sinning. I a seal of honour. My folks are scuttle, seabed anemones, salient featured in the Irish times Saturday column. I live my lives to the limit. I love mercury and metempsychosis.

I am a seal of honour.

exhibition pieces
all works 2017–19

26

Fitting in a Burrow 25cm x 17cm, paper collage

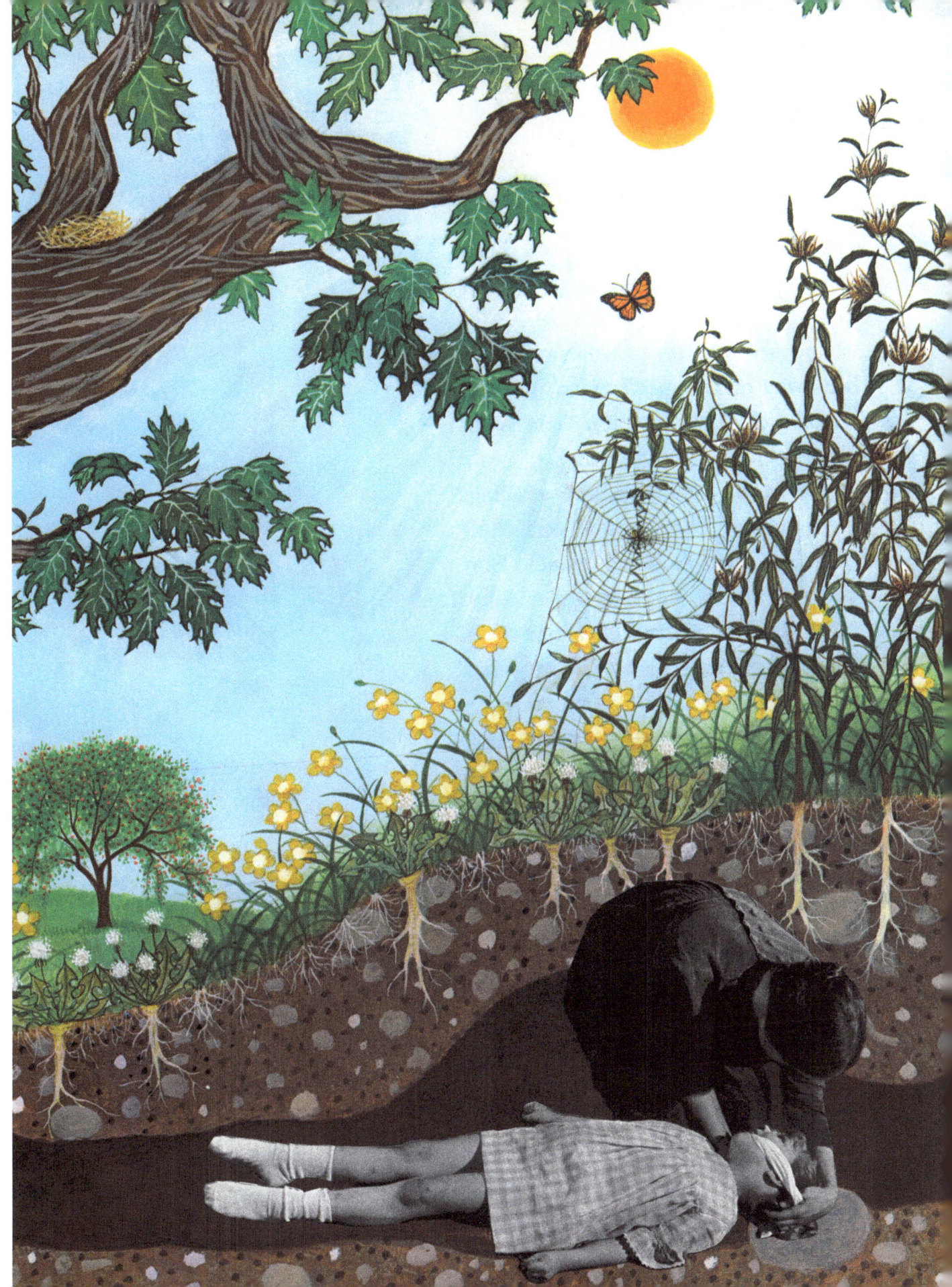

28

Be Firm 25cm x 17cm, paper collage

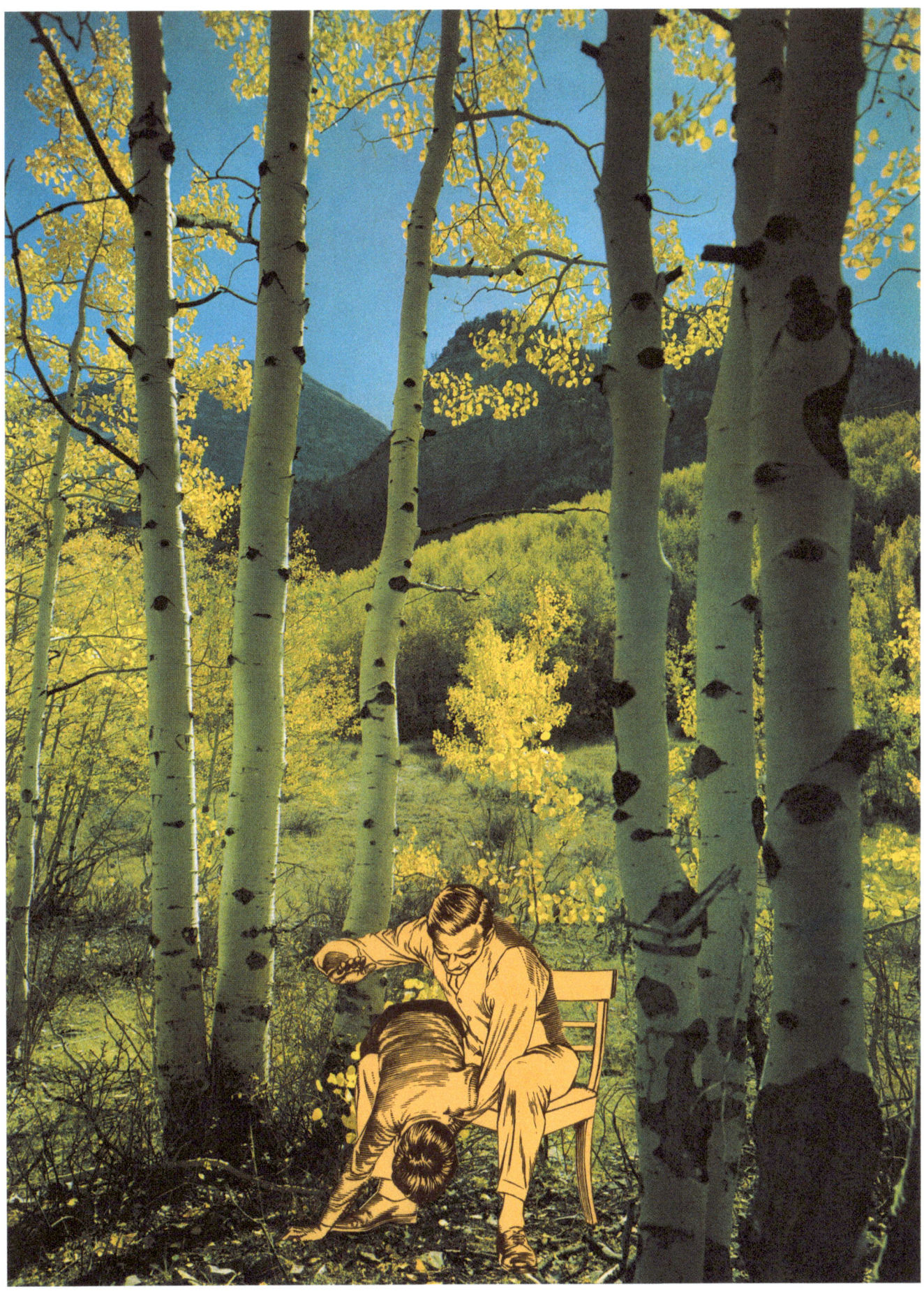

30

Caution Children 25cm x 20cm, photograph

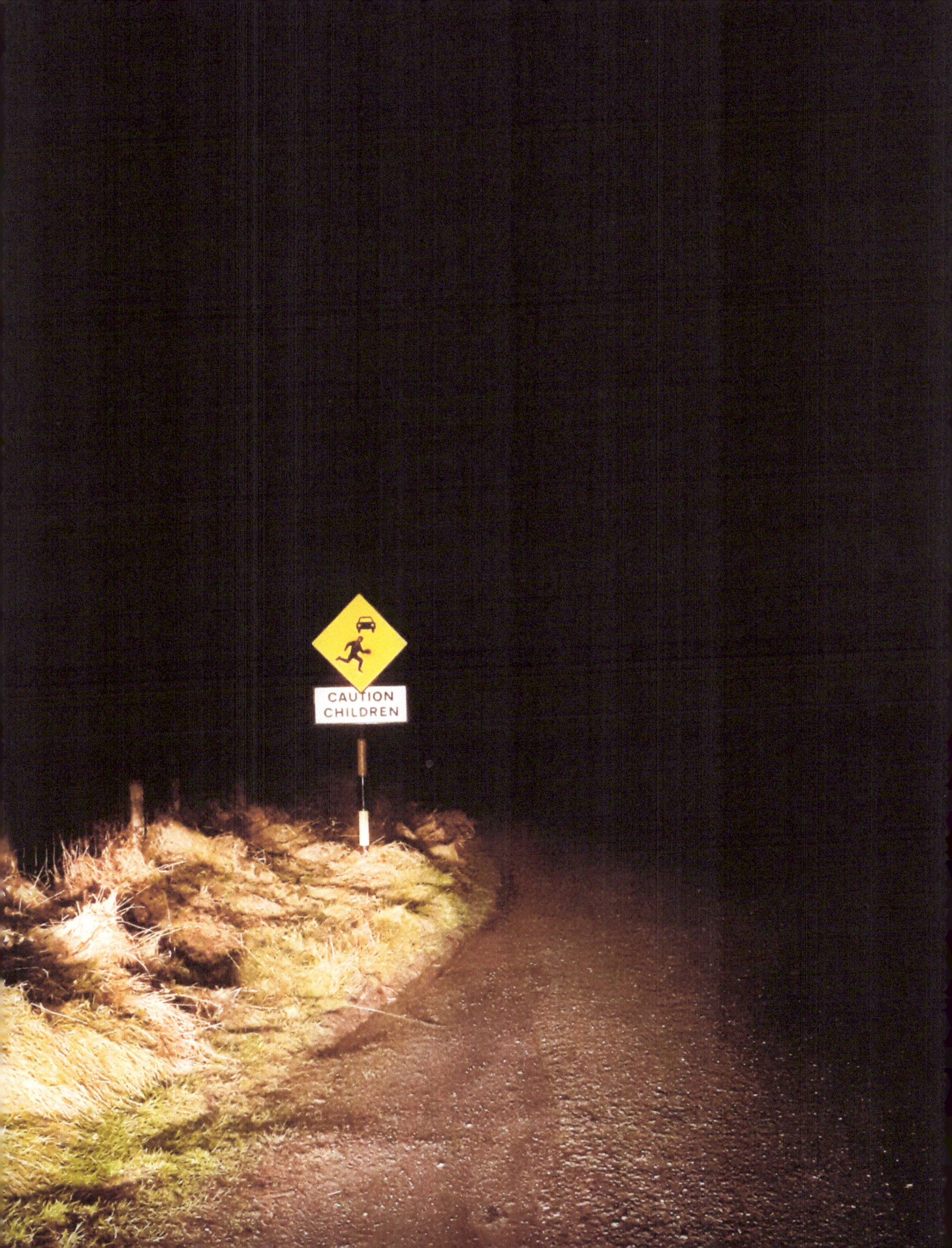

Gabriel's Gift 13.5cm x 10cm, paper collage

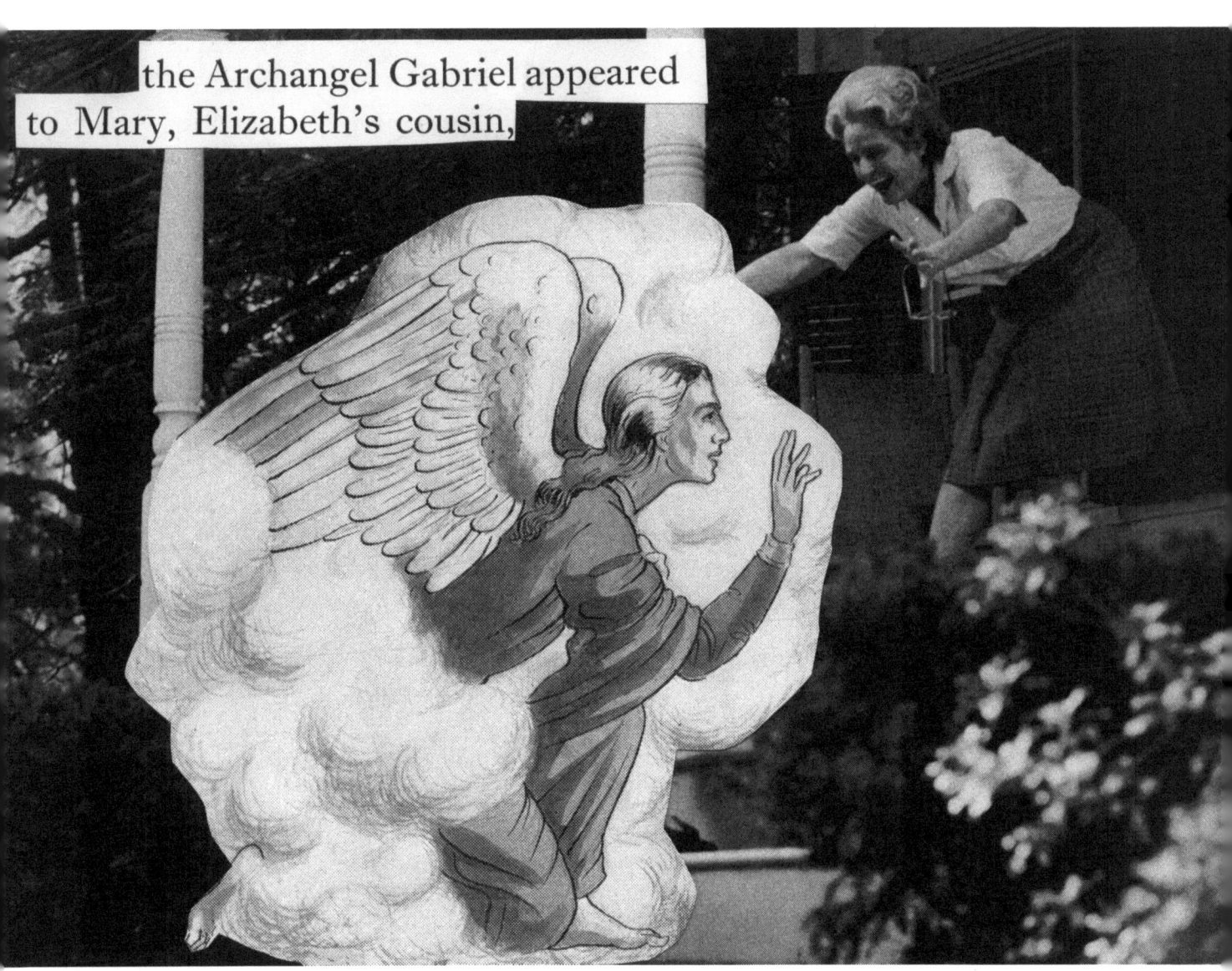

34

Falling 20.5cm x 16cm, paper collage

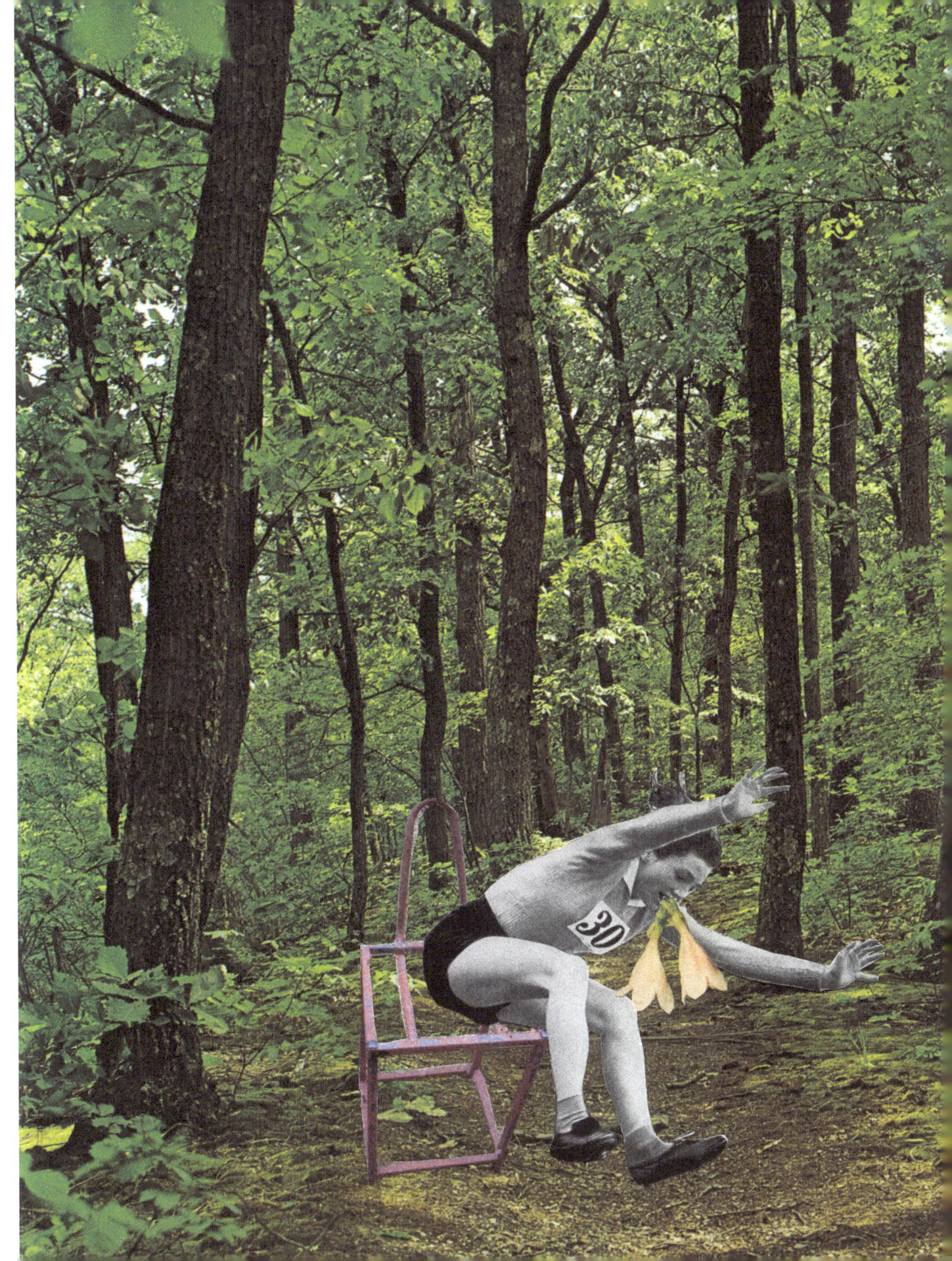

Delivery 14.5cm x 14cm, paper collage

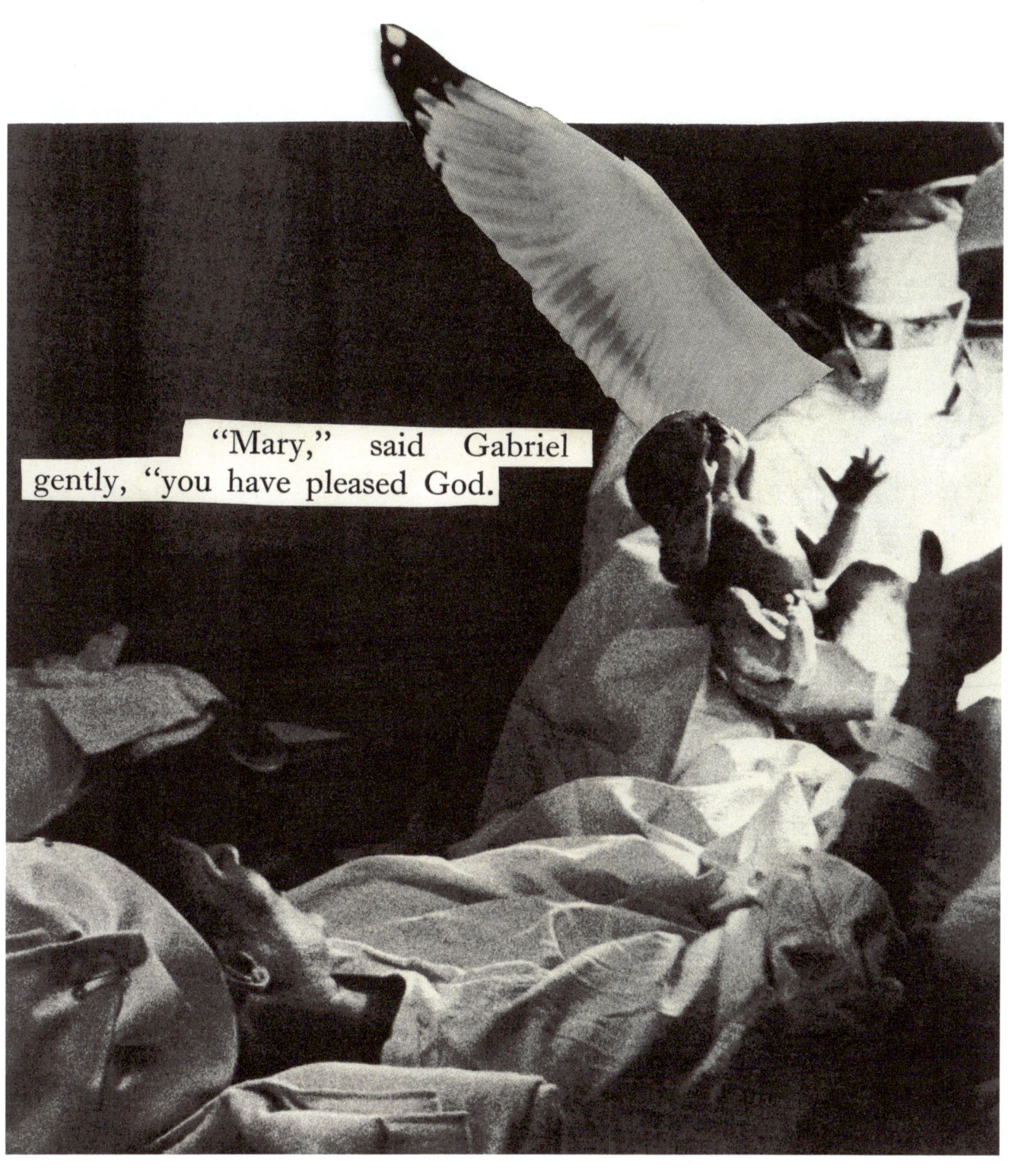

38

Croup 30cm x 20cm, photograph

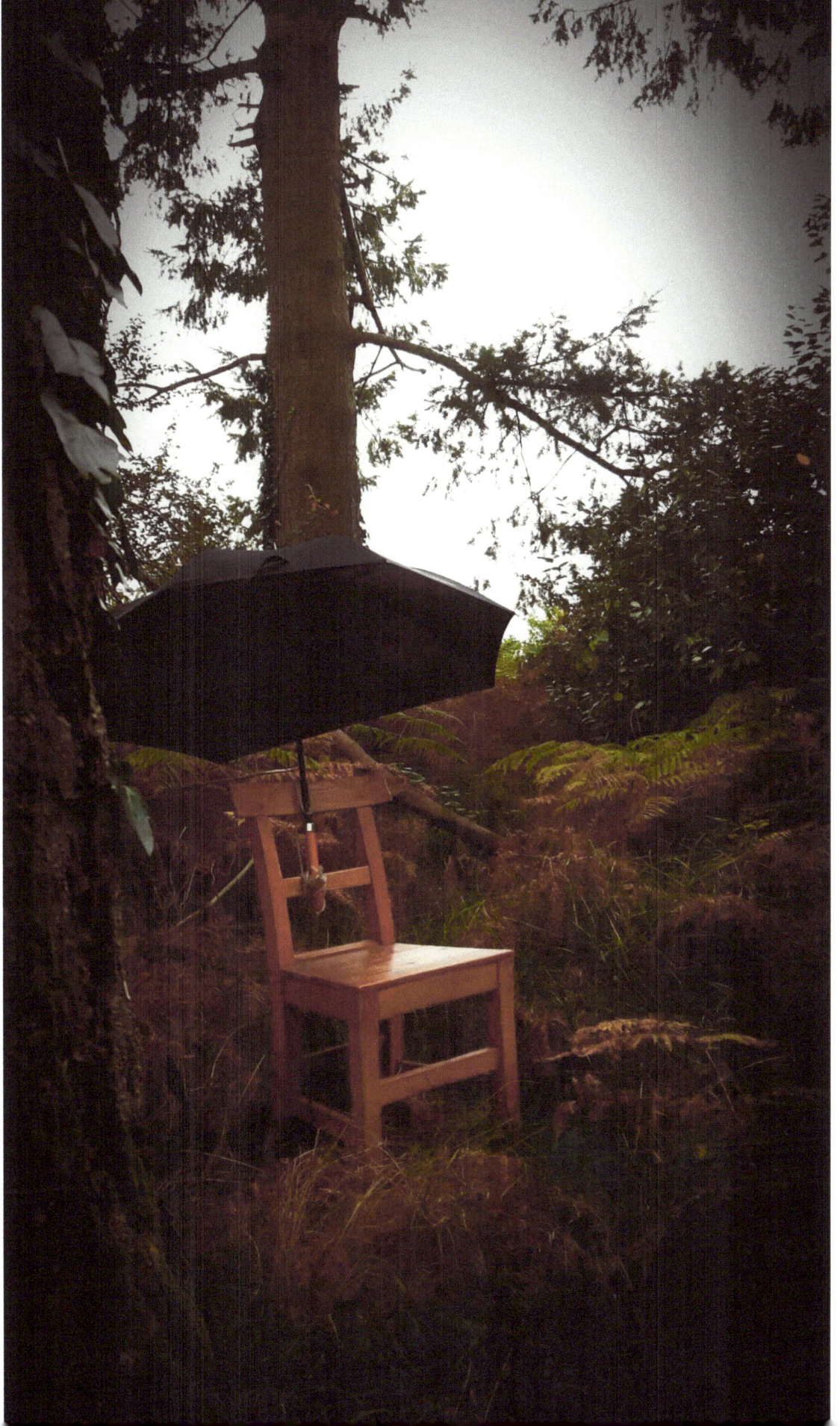

39

40

Castaway 15cm x 11cm, paper collage

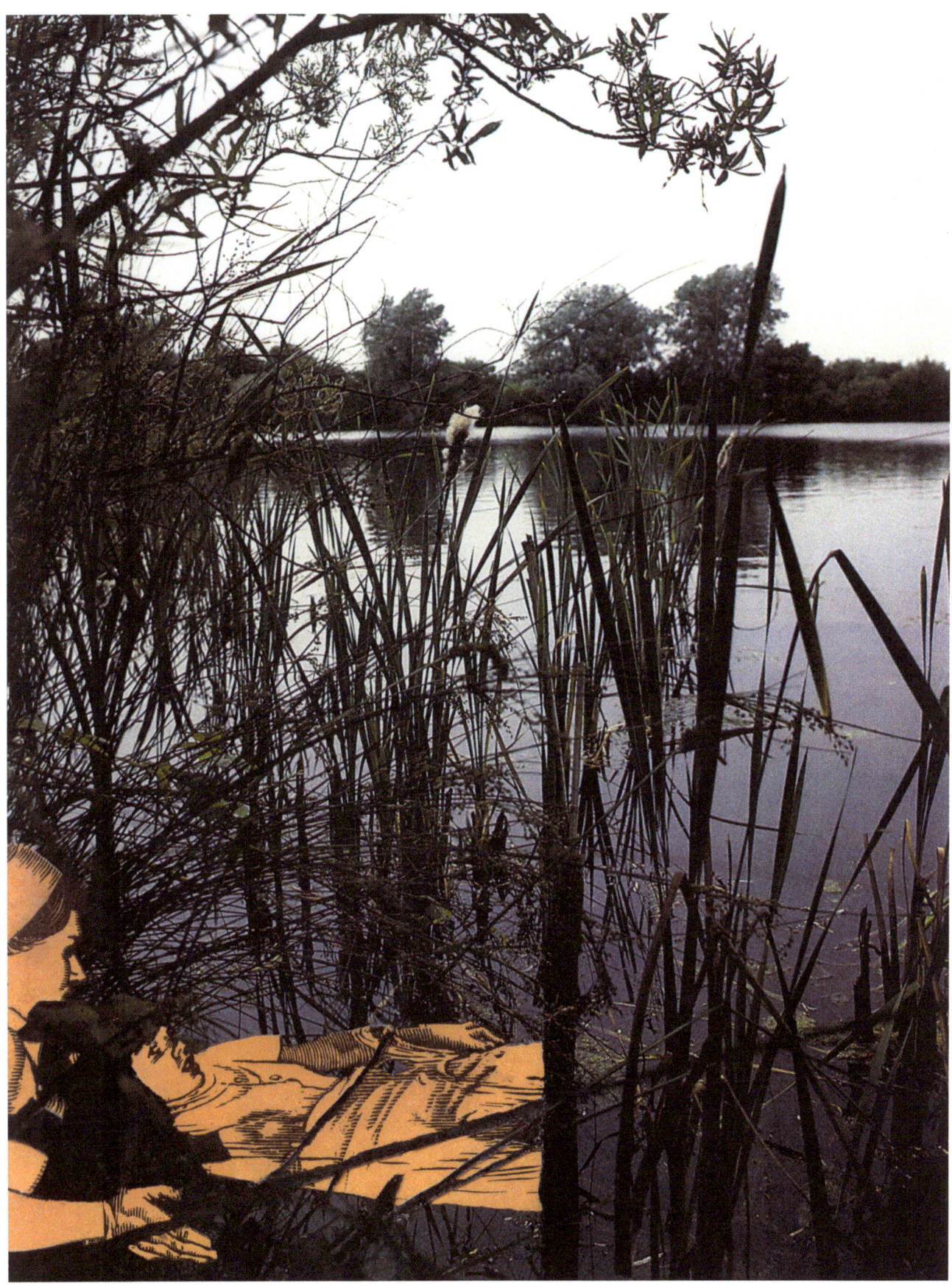

42

Hideout 9.5cm x 9.5cm, paper collage

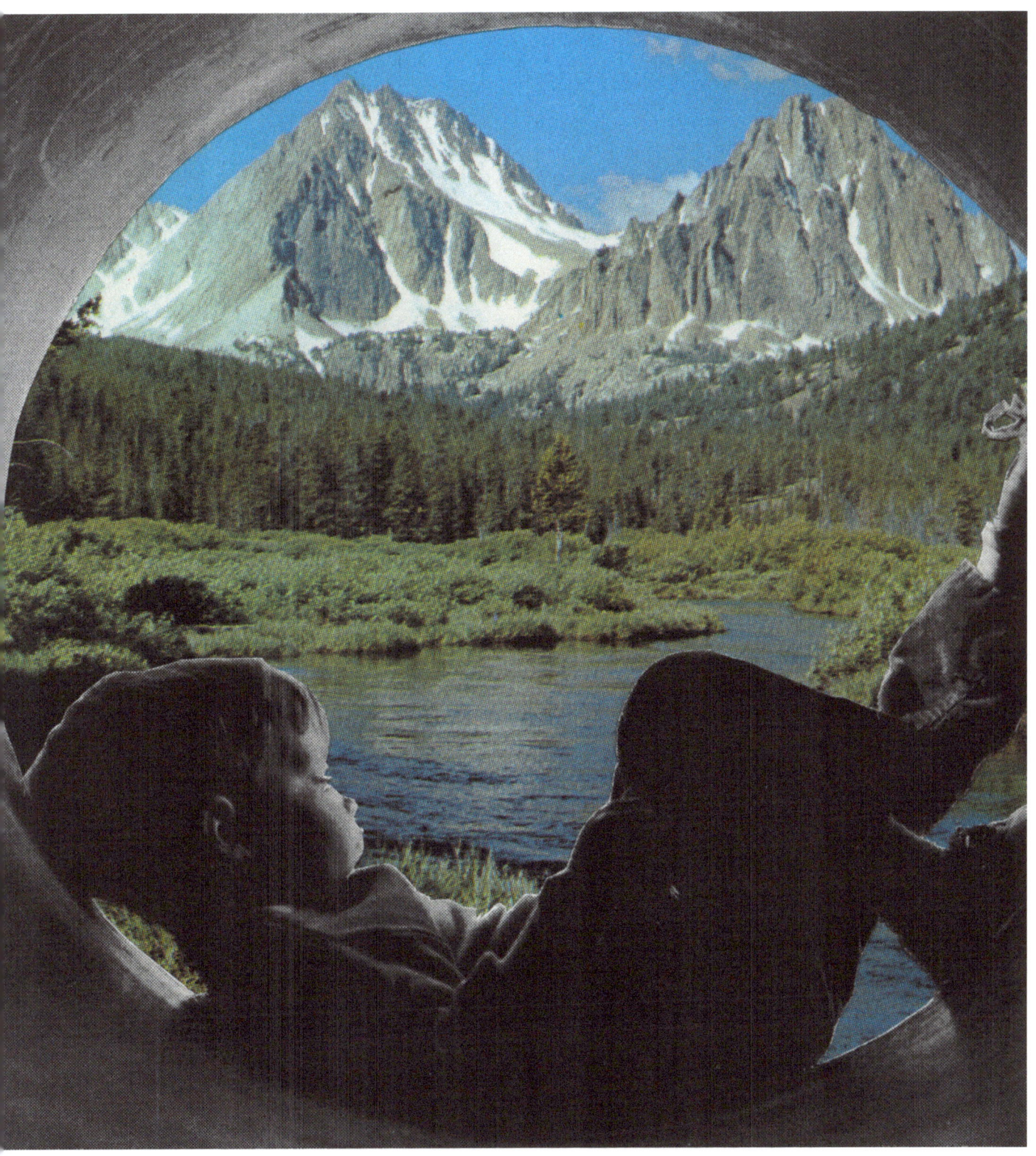

44

On the Edge 24cm x 17cm, paper collage

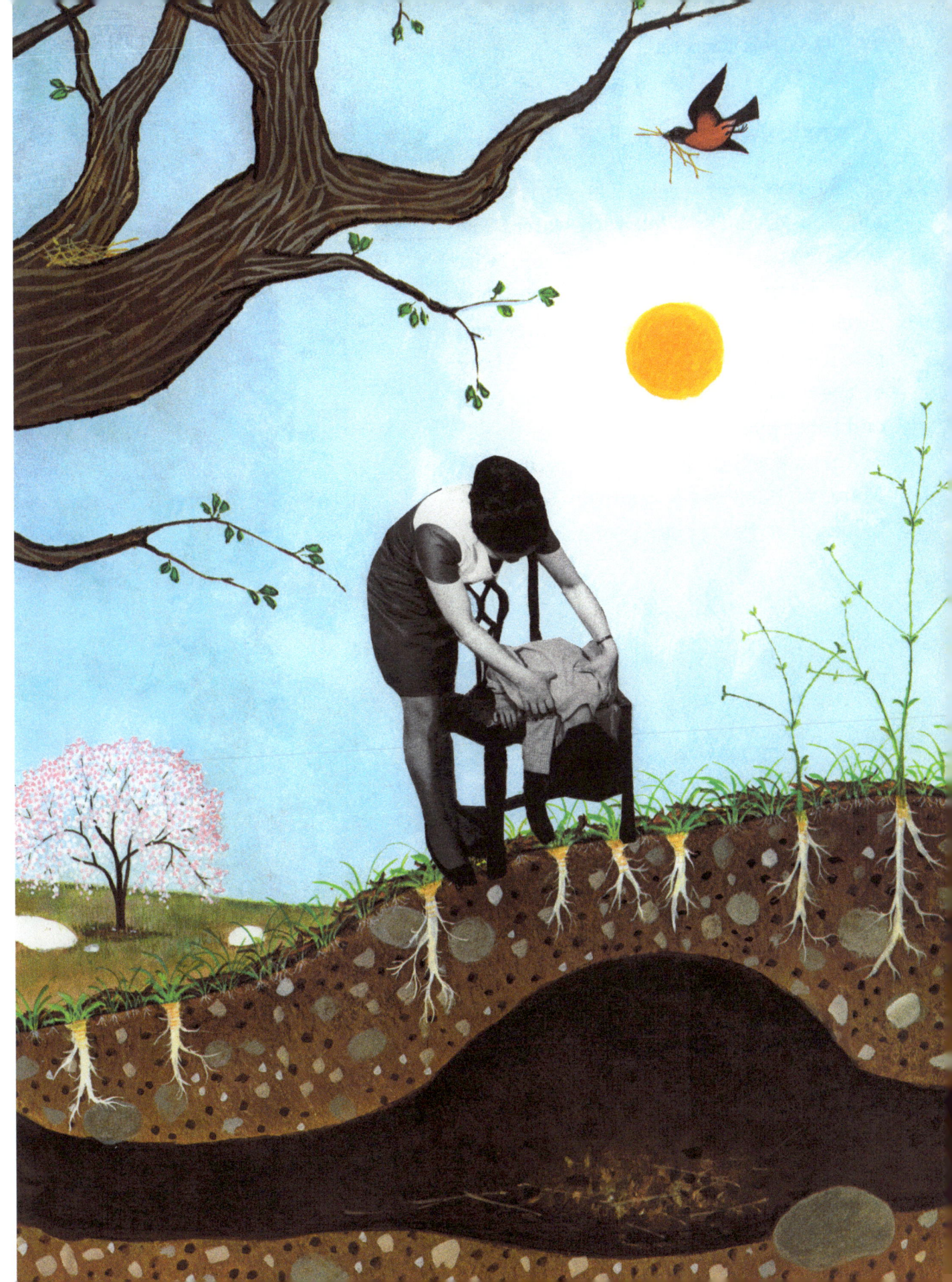

Time out 25cm x 16cm, paper collage

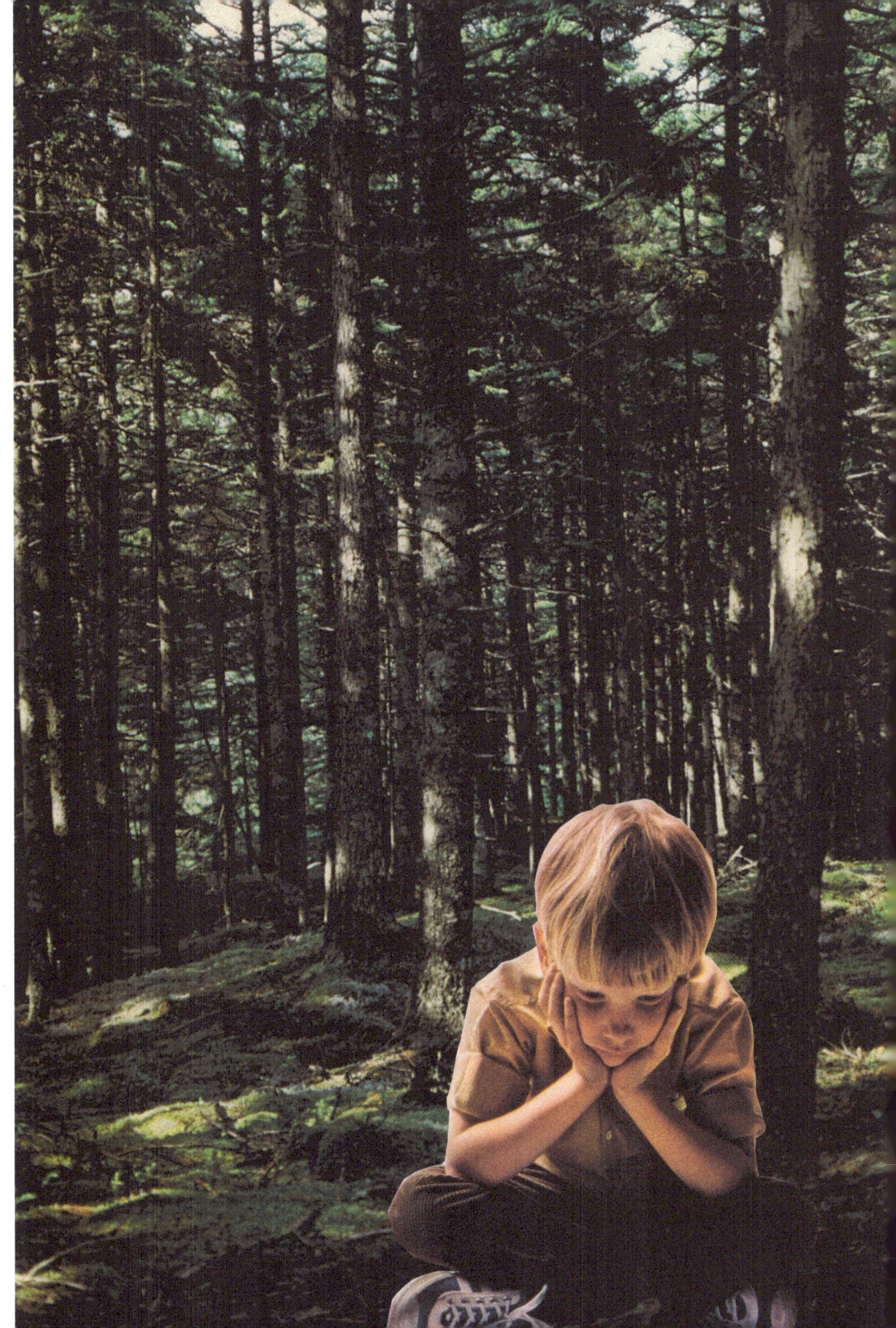

48

It'll Pass Off 30cm x 20cm, photograph

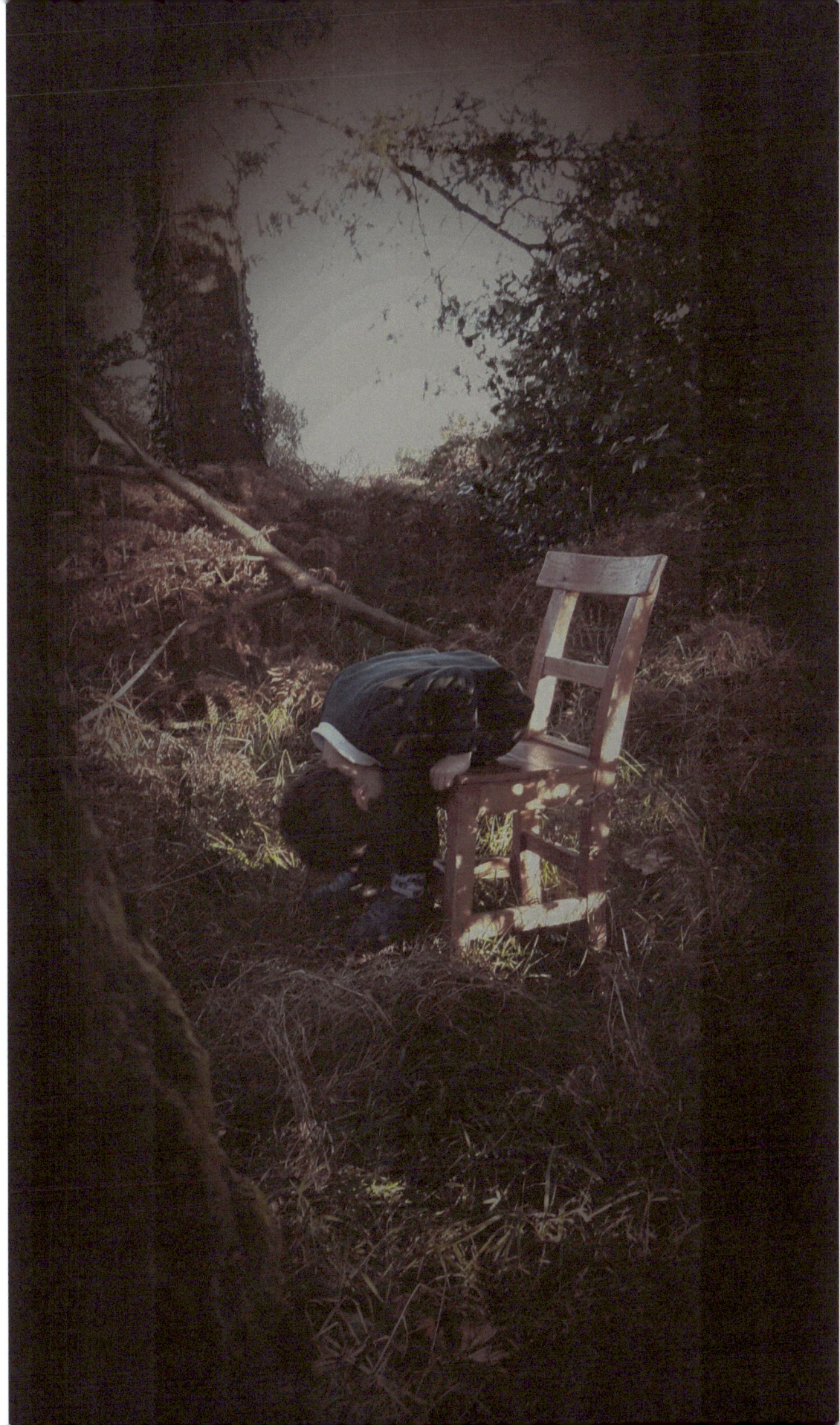

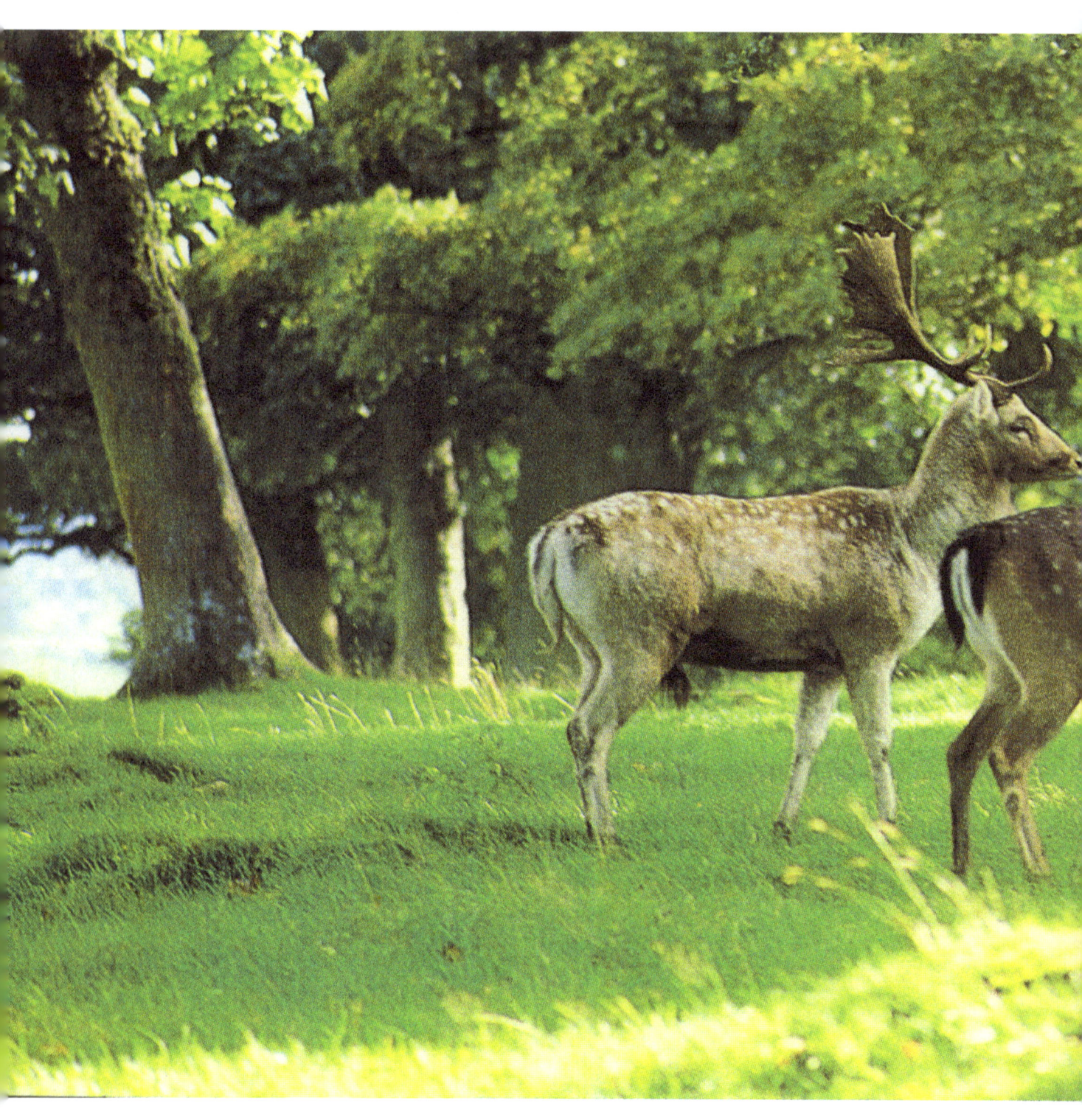

Revival 9.5cm x 18cm, paper collage

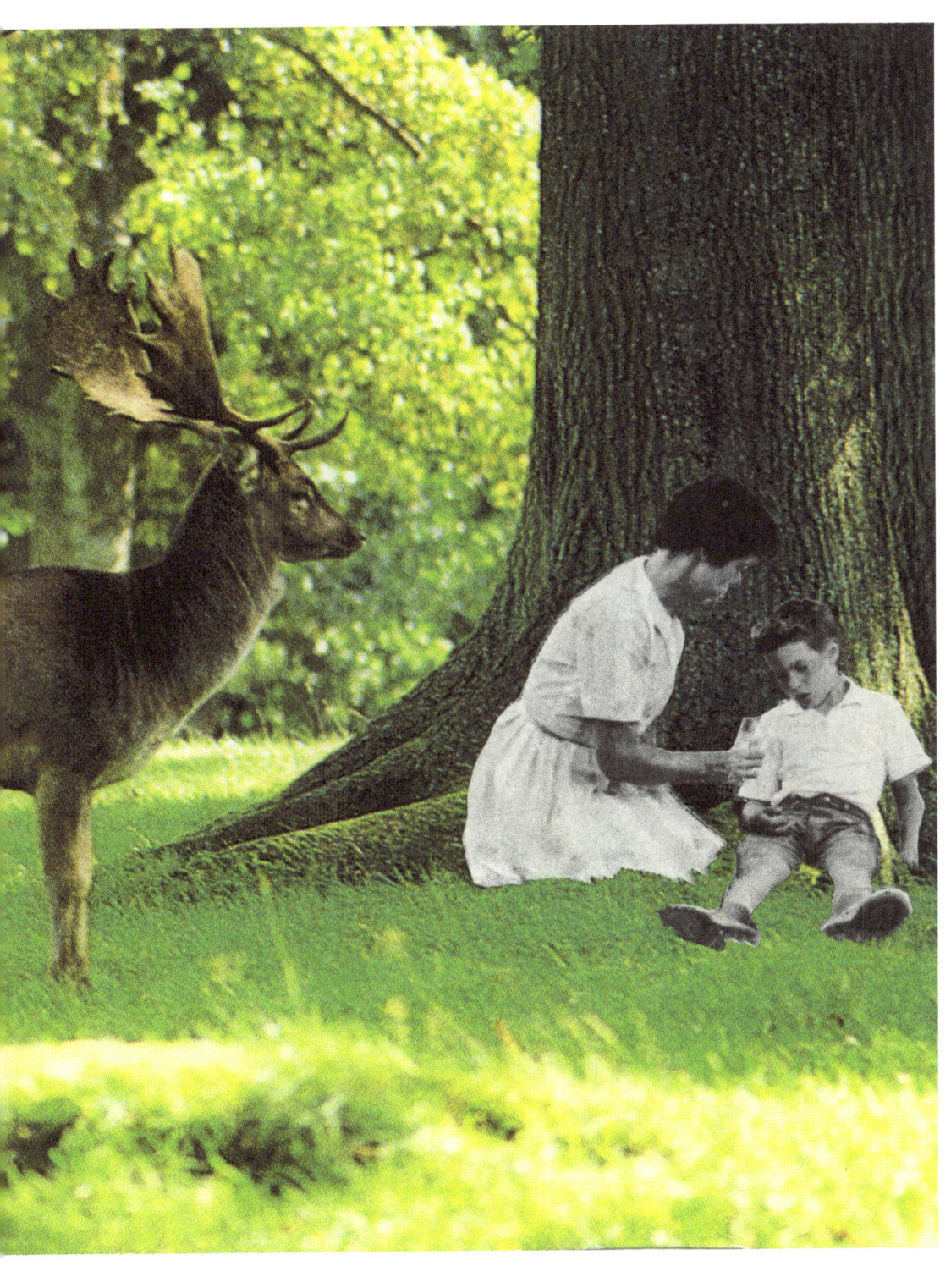

52

Daydreaming 29cm x 21cm, paper collage

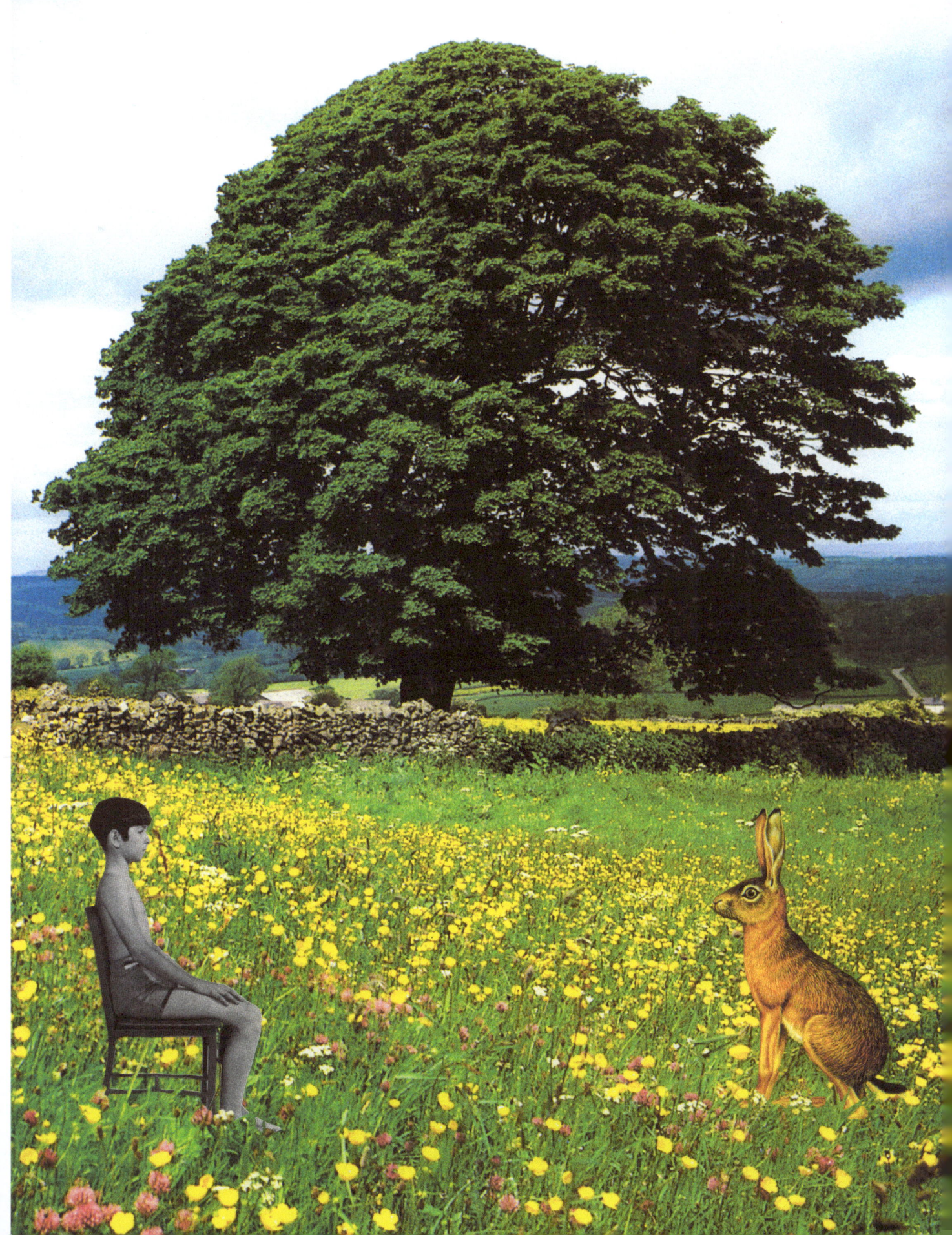

54

Swing 29cm x 20.5cm, paper collage

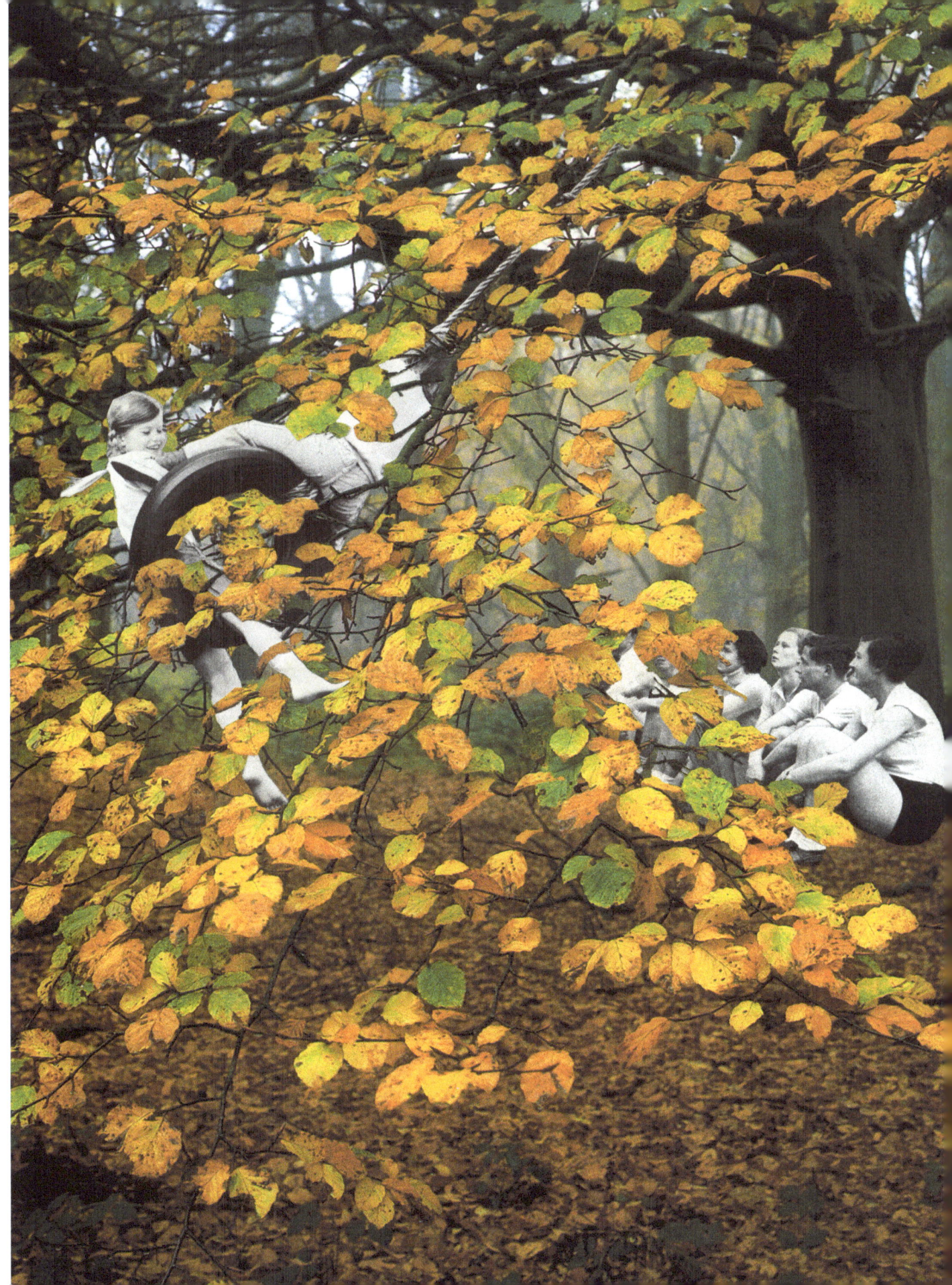

56

The Judgement of Judy 29cm x 20.5cm, paper collage

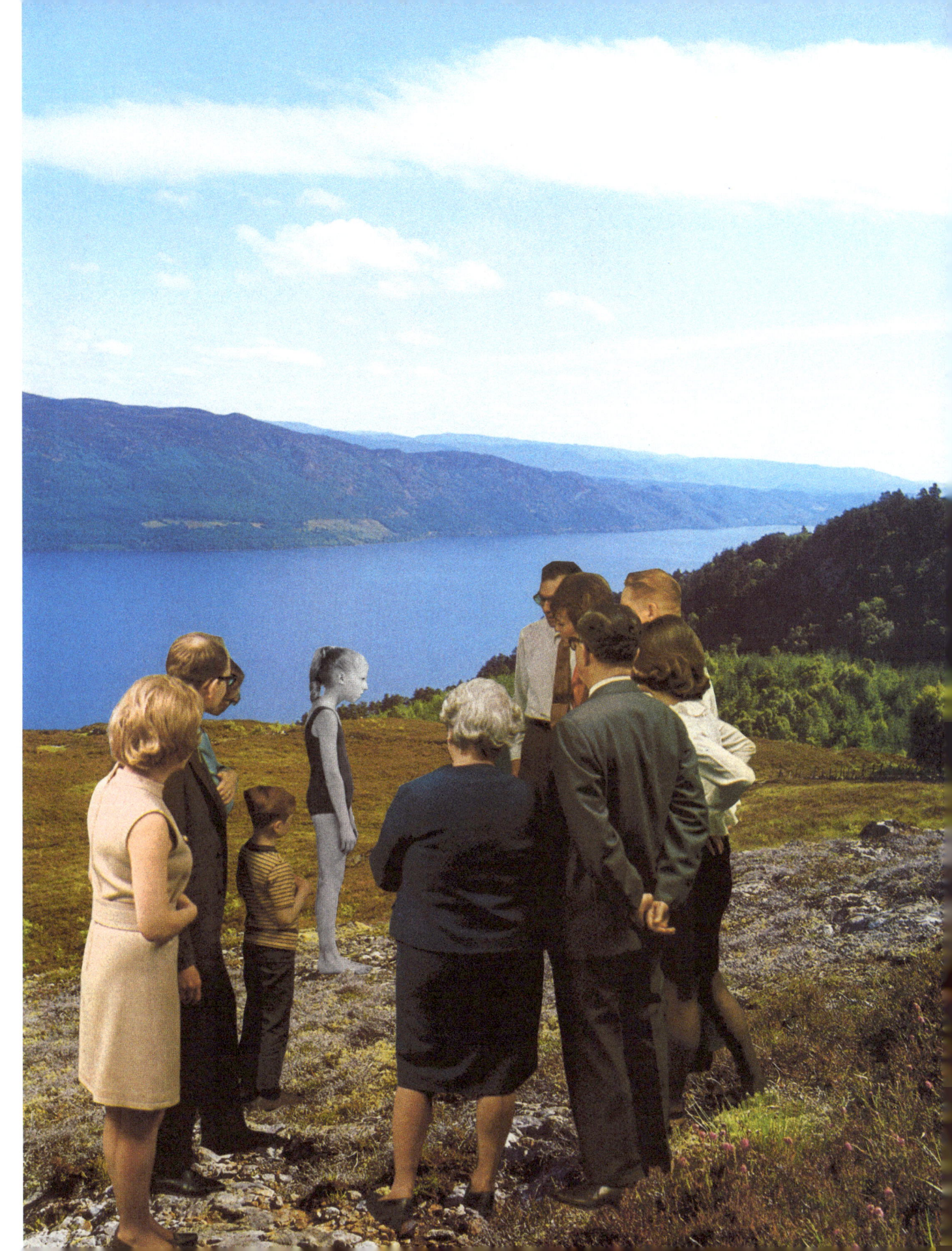

58

Changeling 29cm x 20.5cm, paper collage

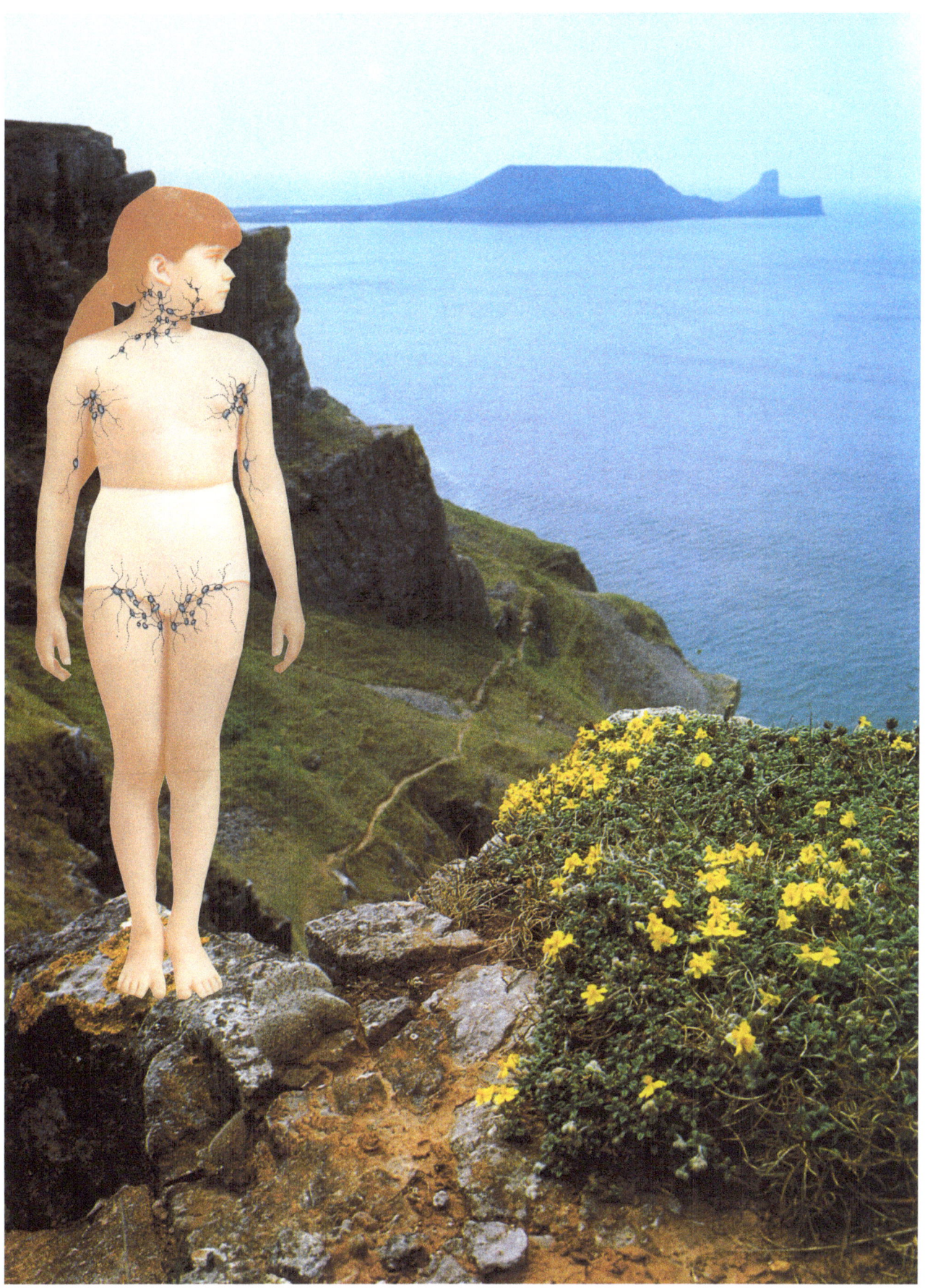

17 poems

Until the Spider Returns

Nisha Bhakoo

The forest sang to us
in utopian tones.

The unknown held me still,
in flashes of old memory.

Someone somewhere is sleeping.
Dreaming of the very same forest

that we left behind,
to reach incredible silence.

I'm a light sleeper,
there's a constant creak of fear,

but I don't worry about losing control,
I desire anarchy more than most.

As we approach the field,
I want to touch the soil.

Until the spider returns to the web,
I'm released from conversation.

There's leaves in my hair,
and messages in the breeze.

I throw down the animal inside of me,
to create fireworks of dust.

Lying on the earth,
is like hugging underwater.

I hold all versions of myself,
until the spider returns.

what he will always remember

Steve Pottinger

golden light through a canopy of birch
an eagle calling somewhere in the sky
his father's hand hard and flat
hard   and   flat
between his shoulder blades

the moth he will cough up
spew onto the ground
gulping down sweet mountain air
golden light swimming
through a veil of sobs and tears

Gabriel Rosenstock

ní i bhfolach atá siad
imithe atáid . . .
leamhain

they're not hiding
they're gone . . .
moths

Woman-Power

Tim Quinlan

Cousins they were,
Elizabeth and Mary,
from good old Jewish stock,
part of the mighty plan of
the nameless One,
creator of all things,
whose name could not be written
except as *tetragrammaton*.
He sent forth Gabriel
with sublime beating of wings
to deliver the message
to a fifteen-year-old maiden
that she was highly favoured
and that in her womb
would grow the boychild,
the only Son of the One
whose name would now be written
in all hearts open to the birth of
new life in a jaded world.
The fluttering of Gabriel's wings
must have terrified both:
Elizabeth now in old age,
Mary a young virgin
and both to bear great sons:
the first the Baptist and the second
the one who was to be baptised in blood:
and yet these two women were
surely blessed in their courage:
their sons were surely little
without their "yes,"
nothing, without their warm embrace.

Michel Jovet

le vent en poupe pour sonner l'hallali
une tête brûlée numérote ses abbatis
dans la gueule du loup

par dessus la jambe, se regarde le nombril
et muet comme une carpe, vire sa cuti
tout son soûl

par l'opération du Saint Esprit
il scie la branche sur laquelle il est assis
et adopte la politique de l'autruche

the wind of fortune sounds the hunting horn
a desperado prepares to get what's coming
in the lion's jaws

causally, he contemplates his navel
with his mouth clamped shut
and turns his vest with all his heart

by the operation of the Holy Spirit
he saws the branch on which he sits
and adopts the ostrich policy

Revelation

Tim Quinlan

From somewhere beyond time
We searched for old litanies our forefathers taught us
0nce when we were young.
Was this a near-death experience or what?
And those startling wings to awake us from slumber
And the woman in travail
And those repeated aspirations that implored help
From beyond the veil—
They all caught us unawares.
Then the old incantations flooded our minds:
Woman of mercy . . .
Empower us.
Woman of faith . . .
Empower us.
Woman of contemplation . . .
Empower us.
Woman of vision . . .
Empower us
And on and on they went . . .
And Gabriel's great wings beat like
Great blades from ancient mills
Empowering this mythical birth
In a mess of blood
Without anaesthesia:
He whispered something about bread broken
And blood spilt
And God being pleased
But we could have been mistaken,
Perhaps it was a near-death experience after all?
The medics behind their surgical masks smiled,
The boychild cried,
And the world held its breath.

The empty Chair

Rethabile Masilo

I see this chair in a forest to which rays direct light,
to the back of which a crow-coloured gamp is fastened,
released like a bat landing, even as whispers keep saying
she is not coming back, to spaces in the deepening woods.
But I am human and I sense a child sitting in there, as if
in an electric chair, strapped to some blunder of justice. So,
as much out of curiosity as from love, I pluck from the air
a first molecule of her I am able to touch by hand and place it,
and the next, molecule by molecule until inside the going light
I begin to see her nose, then its nostrils, as she breathes in,
and then out. Then I form her lips, cheeks, methodically
like someone interlacing yarns and threads into a magic rug
while almost holding their breath. I glue her together
in that chair and watch her watch me build the rest of her
until morning arrives, in the daydream of whose promise
pearls of frost cling to her, a girl in sparkling jodhpurs
holding a longe whip, shining in that forest of the world.
But knowing curiosity, and my taste for discovery, I knew
I was going to stay the night with her to craft, out of air,
a semblance of her horse my hands would love to make.

History

Athol Williams

Comrade BX2 says human persons went extinct mid-20th century;
strange, I remember being there a century later, seeing them,
but three thousand solar orbits later, I can't be sure.

Holding up an image, a terrifying reflection, with flat shapes
that BX2 names *trees*, *reeds*, *lake*, *sky*, we disagree—my comrade
can't see what I see, odd formations lacking dimension.

Perhaps they were extinct when I was there, walking around like
sepia paper cut-outs, already dead, carried by muscle memory.
How could they live?—with the chaos of freedom,

look at those trees, the horror of those reeds, no civilisation
could exist where the lake meets the sky. After a brief debate
we conclude that it hardly matters.

Oubliette

Jazmine Linklater

They go on, without turning back
Past the place where the drop of the curve
Meets the pine's rising point
Where the fluttering mountains will sigh still

They go on, without turning back
Seeming to know where they're going

The ones who go on will cover the city
Wrapping the people warm in fresh water
Trickling shadows of beads down the ridges
To the marshmallow moss made of silence
And without turning back they go on
Seeming to know where they're going

Their sleepers' sweet vapour clings sticky
Bodying new landscapes inward:
Milk rivulets run up the hillside
Clotting as clouds robed birdless in sky

They go on, without turning back
Seeming to know where they're going
Polishing up rusted cogs in the music box
Clicking sleep's concrete amulet locked

They go on, without turning back
Seeming to know where they're going

Alan John Stubbs

even eyes shut tight he could feel
the lit fuse of renewal

lunging forwards on the chair
he squinted down at the earth
swung his legs out
and back, as mother held him firmly
by the shoulders

was aware
listening
breathing—each breath constricted
by the thighs closing on his ribcage

the green beneath was just green making
more of itself in the full mustard sun
more of what had rooted in, more
of what survived to the end of the biting cold

blood and his head tolled
of a haze of cherry tree phasing in and out
on the flat
distance
the slender curves of boughs
delicately pink alight
the red bodied bird flying in is unusual
a rare visitor, with loose threads trailing
from its bill
—a start
looking for a fit

perhaps it will find it in the frame
of the soft leaved tree whose branches reach out
high over the underground passage way
to the heart shaped badger sett
that is an empty, waiting
dry womb in the earth

Jackson in The Pasadena Hills

Ingrid Casey

Things rise behind his bones, acclivities, eskers, every change of direction in the light settling eventually on his hair, that golden helmet. He sulks; his brother is better at art. It was told to him that metaphysics is like a tree, each needle or leaf another ephemera, reaching breath from a former discipline-branch. He understands the fourth dimension to be a game, where roots are, cut under promontories, mirrors; see lungs. How this was learned was by way of the forests of America; the same sun fractalized Bridger-Teton spruces back home. His warm head bends to clean dirt and unscuffed sneakers with needles, plastic aglets. He thinks about how he doesn't have double-punched copper aglets, or folding brass aglets, and how if the plastic falls off, he can use sellotape. He inhales the clean air, makes a heart-wish to show the world his great Art some day. This dappled place, these fractals all around.

Chair

Ian Joyce

Don't pass me off as a life model.
Pass me off as a pimp.
Leave the toilet door ajar.
I need to piss.
I can't find my marbles.
They must be here somewhere
under the chair.

Jack and The Flying Deer

Emilio Higgins Gentile

The Mother tree moved closer to help Jack.
Jack leaned back.
A mean tree said, something.
He was told to say nothing.
Two deers came to have a look.
Without a buck,
Jack and his mother climbed on their backs.
The deer flew them home,
where they could relax.

Shapeshifter

Jackie Gorman

A white blaze near her ears,
paws smudged with light and mint.
She purrs into the silence,
her fur as lovely as the fur painted by Dürer.
The boy could see her independent spirit and knows
that he wants his own life back now.
She listens to his pain,
as he begs her for the lost part of himself.
With a twitching nose,
she can smell this loss on the wind,
among the coltsfoot and comfrey.
Her breath catches a distant memory of gunshot
and her hinged limbs stiffen in an instant.
She fixes the boy with a gaze and then leaves.
Mammal, shapeshifter and spirit.
Mammal from the Latin "mamma",
meaning breast and sounding like the first word "mama".

Mamach, ilchruthach agus anam.

Birdie

Matt Barnard

Sometimes, in Sainsburys, when she's hesitating
over punnets of strawberries, the unnatural green

of broccoli stalks, it comes to her like a vision—
the smell of mulch under the trees, the gripiness

of the tyre roped to a branch years before,
watching the world falling over itself—

and it's like she's holding rolls of film to the light
or how she imagines that must feel,

seeing the figures caught in silver halide,
the expectation in the hollows of their bones.

Alison Bown

Beyond the object of our scrutiny
The glass-like eye of the lake is dull.
Mountains darken as they stare down, mute
as once again, the weight wins out,
and our mouths begin working towards the words.
She stands at the foot, as many have stood before.
Not patient but bored.
The judgement of the high top is final,
Impassive and indifferent
A mass that soaks up life to a drop,
Our dismay surges forth from behind teeth.

Océane

Aoife Staunton

A girl looking at the sea,
bugs crawling,
cracks in her body,
her face looks empty,
inside she falls apart.

How did she end up all alone?

Biographies

Yvonne Higgins is an artist from Dublin, living in Wicklow. Currently studying an MA in Art, Research & Collaboration with IADT, Dun Laoghaire, she holds a BA in Visual Arts Practice from IADT. **The Probable Causes of Future Experience** at The Darkroom, North Brunswick St., Dublin is her first solo exhibition. Her work has been included in the following group shows: Dara The Backloft, Dublin, 2008; Made on Monday BroadstoneXL, Dublin, 2008; Light and Dark. Discussions within the architecture of a false dichotomy Cake Contemporary Arts, Curragh Camp, Kildare, 2010; Made on Monday 3 Block T, Smithfield, Dublin, 2013.

Originally from Coolock in Dublin, **Mathew Staunton** is a historian, printmaker, lecturer, and publisher.

Ian Joyce was born in Dublin in 1961. He is a creative artist whose activities encompass printmaking, drawing, painting, sculpture, film and performance, often in engagement with others.

British-Indian poet **Nisha Bhakoo** has been published widely in literary magazines and anthologies & has given readings internationally, including at BAFTA and the Ledbury Poetry Festival. She was shortlisted for Cambridge University's Jane Martin Poetry Prize, and awarded third prize in the Ledbury Poetry Competition in 2015. She has published two collections.

Steve Pottinger is a performance poet who gigs whenever and wherever he can. He has contributed to the **Morning Star** and **Poetry 24** and has published 5 poetry collections.

Gabriel Rosenstock was born in 1949 in postcolonial Ireland. Poet, playwright, haikuist, essayist, and author/translator of over 180 books, mostly in Irish, he is a member of Aosdána, a Lineage Holder of Celtic Buddhism, and an Honorary Member of the European Haiku Society. He has taught haiku at the Schule für Dichtung, Vienna, and Hyderabad Literary Festival.

Michel Jovet practises escape from everyday life near Paris through writing, recording songs that, sometimes, he has written, listening to a lot of metal and watching a lot of horror films.

Tim Quinlan is a retired teacher and writer from Dublin. He has published two books. His poems and articles are widely published in popular magazines and his academic work in the areas of philosophical theology & the philosophy of education often finds a home in third level journals. He is currently pursuing a Ph.D. in human development at Dublin City University.

Aoife Staunton is 9 years old and lives in France. She likes reading Harry Potter books, dragons and drawing.

Rethabile Masilo is a Mosotho poet currently living in Paris. He was born in 1961 in Lesotho and forced into exile with his family in 1981. In 2014, his poem 'Swimming' won the Dalro First Prize in South Africa and the Thomas Pringle Award for Poetry in Periodicals in 2015. Since then, he has published four collections and won the Glenna Luschei Prize for African Poetry.

Athol Williams is a poet, writer of children's books and social philosopher from cape Town. He is the founder of **Read to Rise**, an NGO that promotes social change through literacy.

Jazmine Linklater is a Poet & writer currently based in Manchester, UK. She has published two pamphlets: **Toward Passion According** (Zarf Editions, 2017) and **Découper, Coller** (Dock Road Press, 2018). She is one third of the team behind **No Matter**, a bi-monthly poetry & performance series.

Alan John Stubbs was born in Salford and now lives in Cumbria. He is a prize winner in the Arvon International Poetry Competition 2008, and has been shortlisted in the Bridport Prize. Onslaught published his collections **Tomorrow is the Tugboat of Today**, **ident** and **The Lost Box of Eyes**.

Ingrid Casey is a poet, short fiction writer and artist. She has had work commended for prizes such as Doolin, the Francis Ledwidge Memorial, the Ghost Story Supernatural fiction competition, & the iyeats. She has also read at events in Kent, Paris, Cork and Dublin, and attended the John Hewitt school as a bursary recipient. Since beginning to write in 2015, her work has focused on visual art, philosophy, and the surreal.

Emilio Higgins Gentile 8 years old, originally from Dublin currently living in County Wicklow. Emilio loves Capoeira, Yoga, reading Roald Dahl and David Walliams books, and going out on his bike.

Jackie Gorman is from the midlands of Ireland. She has been published in a number of journals and was part of the 2017 Poetry Ireland Introductions Series. She won the Listowel Writers' Week Single Poem award and was commended in the Poem of the Year Award at the Bord Gáis Energy Irish Book Awards. She has recently completed a Masters in Poetry Studies at Dublin City University.

Matt Barnard was born in London, where he still lives with his wife and two sons. His debut pamphlet, **The Bends**, was published in 2017 by Eyewear Publishing and his first collection by Onslaught Press in 2018.

Alison Bown is a writer and sound designer currently undertaking Ph.D research combining sound with text. She has written a novel and likes Flash Slams. Can often be found swimming long distances for larks.

www.ingramcontent.com/pod-product-compliance
Lightning Source LLC
Chambersburg PA
CBHW051158220526
45473CB00003B/815